SINGLE PARENTING IN THE 21ST CENTURY AND BEYOND: A SINGLE MOTHER'S GUIDE TO REARING SONS WITHOUT FATHERS

Dr. Josef A. Passley

Note for Librarians: A cataloguing record for this book is available from Library and Archives Canada at www.collectionscanada.ca/amicus/index-e.html
ISBN 1-4251-0358-8

Printed in Victoria, BC, Canada. Printed on paper with minimum 30% recycled fibre. Trafford's print shop runs on "green energy" from solar, wind and other environmentally-friendly power sources.

Offices in Canada, USA, Ireland and UK

Book sales for North America and international:
Trafford Publishing, 6E–2333 Government St.,
Victoria, BC V8T 4P4 CANADA
phone 250 383 6864 (toll-free 1 888 232 4444)
fax 250 383 6804; email to orders@trafford.com

Book sales in Europe:
Trafford Publishing (UK) Limited, 9 Park End Street, 2nd Floor
Oxford, UK OX1 1HH UNITED KINGDOM
phone +44 (0)1865 722 113 (local rate 0845 230 9601)
facsimile +44 (0)1865 722 868; info.uk@trafford.com

Order online at:
trafford.com/06-2115

10 9 8 7 6 5 4 3

DEDICATION

To my wife, parents, and brothers who have been so instrumental in my personal and professional successes. And to my aunts, Eva Biggerstaff and Florence Passley, who, due to their passing this year, were not able to see the completion of this book. I was blessed to have their consistent support and prayers throughout my life.

ACKNOWLEDGEMENTS

I would like to first thank God who has blessed me in more ways than I could ever imagine. I am grateful to my wife Staci who has been a great support to me during the writing and revising of this book. I thank you for your patience and encouragement.

I would also like to thank my parents, Dr. Harold and Yvonne Passley who taught me from childhood to never give up on my dreams and to aim high. They believed I could achieve even before I did. Their words of wisdom, motivation, and guidance have been instrumental in who I am today.

I would also like to make special mention of Mary McClurkin, who helped me in the editing of this book. Many thanks as well to Carol Coleman and Raymond Woods for giving me the opportunity to talk on the radio to a larger audience about topics such as the special needs of single mothers. Lastly, I want to thank Drs. Joan Gerring and Arlene Gerson for their wise mentoring throughout the course of my career.

SINGLE PARENTING IN THE 21ST CENTURY AND BEYOND

- **Was written** for single women like you who live with the challenges of raising a male child in the 21st century
- **Will help** you to develop effective communication to strengthen your mother/son relationship
- **Will show** you ways to help you become a better, happier, more successful parent of your son

CONTENTS

FOREWORD

The successful treatment of boys with behavior problems from the youngest ages to the teenage years is an enormous challenge to everyone involved in the care of these children. Aggression in youth is a major public health problem in this country because of the large numbers of children involved and the great burden of their behavior on their families and their communities. Boys who do not listen and who are aggressive are the most frequent visitors to child mental health clinics. They obtain help from caring professionals in clinics and in private offices. School teachers and school counselors are also involved in the daily care of these children with behavior problems. But it is the parents who live with their sons and are most involved with them who will have the largest role to play in the day-to-day carrying out of a behavioral plan. Their role is most important and always crucial for success.

Often there is only the mother who is there for the parenting. The task is a large one, and as Dr. Passley clearly points out, raising a son well is a difficult but possible job for a mother to do. In this book, Dr. Passley first lays out the problems and risks that the mother faces in single parenting, but once he describes the situation, he quickly proceeds to provide a simple guide to parenting a boy, giving examples from his clinical practice. He focuses on the absence of the father as the factor that has a profound effect on the son because of his loss that may lead to either anger or depression, and a profound effect on the mother because of her loss of support and companionship. In the context of loss, Dr. Passley supplies motivation and optimism to help the mother build a plan for success for her and her child. Instead of focusing on the sadness and depression a lot of these mothers experience, he takes a positive, interactive solution and encourages the mother to take control of the relationship and to rebuild it in a healthy manner.

Dr. Passley describes from his practice and his

study of the literature parenting practices that have not worked well for the single mother. He moves from these examples to describe more effective ways to handle difficult situations that will lead to an improved and strengthened mother-son relationship. He gives clear and simple rules for effective parenting that the mother can present to her son as rules of the home and that can be implemented quickly because they are easily understood and will not entail lengthy discussion. He helps the mother deal with her own negative feelings so that she can enforce the rules that she has established. He emphasizes that the mother should exert her authority consistently, in a loving and supportive manner. Importantly, Dr. Passley recommends how best to deal with the topic of the absent father when it arises, so that the mother does not contribute to negative feelings that her son may have or involve her son in her own existing conflicts with the father.

Dr. Passley skillfully presents those most important parenting tasks facing the single mother of building self-esteem, establishing boundaries, and establishing male role models for her son. All of his suggestions are easy to understand and within the reach of the mother who is motivated to make some positive changes. All of the recommendations are presented with the assurance that they will work and lead to improvement in the behavior of the boy and his relationship with his mother.

Most mothers struggle with the behavior problems of their sons by themselves and do not bring them to the attention of professionals. Either because the problems are viewed as minor or because these mothers feel authoritarian that the problems will go away or because they do not have the finances to seek mental health attention, these mothers rely on their own resources including family and friends to get them through the crises that may arise with their sons. This book can serve as an excellent resource for these mothers working on their own, as well as for the mothers who have sought the assistance of counselors and doctors to help them to work on their parenting skills.

Dr. Passley has an understanding that stems from his academic interest and from his years of clinical experience as a child psychologist at Johns Hopkins Bayview Medical Center. He directly addresses the single mother and provides her with a recipe to gain control of her family and to maximize its functioning. His underlying goal has always been to improve the mental health of children and families through improvement in the quality of mother-child interactions. Dr. Passley is to be congratulated for his optimistic and forceful presentation of this very important topic of a single mother parenting a son.

Joan P. Gerring, M.D.
Medical Director, Child Services
Associate Professor of Psychiatry and Pediatrics
Johns Hopkins University School of Medicine
Baltimore, Maryland

INTRODUCTION

The media has devoted much attention to the differences between boys' and girls' biological functioning, the ways they are reared, and academic success. A January 2006 *Newsweek* article entitled "The Boy Crisis," for example, examined gender differences and how those differences came into play in the classroom. Similarly, a 2006 PBS documentary called *Raising Cain,* hosted by Michael Thompson, Ph.D., a Harvard psychologist, examined the topic of boys and their biological functioning. In 2001, psychologist Dr. James Dobson published a best-selling book entitled *Bringing up Boys,* which examines boys, their emotional and physical development, and other topics related to raising male children. These and other media coverage about the distinctions between girls and boys showed that a woman raising a boy without a father has a much more difficult task than if she were raising a daughter—or if there were a male in the household to provide guidance and support.

The United States today is the world's leader in father-absent families, a distinction it should not be proud of. As a result, American society has experienced unprecedented challenges in the lack of success of many males and the downward spiral of the male population. In comparison to females, males have higher rates of arrests, incarceration, academic failures, and physical violence altercations. These are only a few of the troubling statistics. I wholeheartedly believe the growing number and kinds of problems experienced by males has to do with the increase of single parent homes. America's rising divorce and separation rates have also driven up the numbers of mothers raising sons alone. There are other causes for a woman having to act as both parents. The father could be in prison or on an extended tour of duty with the military or he may have died. Single mothers do not deliberately create their situation.

My interest in this challenging topic started when I was a graduate student considering dissertation topics. Since much of my caseload and colleagues at Johns Hopkins were comprised of single mothers seeking help, I decided to study the effects of a father's absence on pre-adolescent boys. As I analyzed the data a trend began to emerge. Boys became depressed when their father or father figure was not in the home. The data showed that depression, if not treated, often led to aggression and even violence at a higher rate than those with a father or father figure in the home. As I realized how frustrating it must be for a single mother to raise a son alone, I became truly inspired to help single mothers through this difficult endeavor. I realized through my cases that a single mother was capable of raising a son alone if she had encouragement, support, and knowledge. This book is the result of my research and clinical cases.

I hope this book will help you to improve your relationship with your son and to help you to become the best mother you can be as you guide your son to becoming the best adult he can be. This book also suggests ways to make your own life fuller. If you can develop a satisfactory life for yourself, your son will be better for it.

These pages include information I have learned not only from formal training and study, but from interventions I have used successfully to treat the hundreds of single mothers and their sons I have counseled throughout the years. Parenthood under ideal conditions is not easy, but a single mother raising a boy needs many more skills to ease her burden of being the sole disciplinarian, provider, and guide for her child. I hope you find this book as a great benefit for you and your family.

Josef A. Passley, Ph.D.

1

SINGLE MOTHERS AND SONS: CRITICAL CHALLENGES

In 2000, there were more than 10 million single-mother families with children under the age of 18 in the United States, and if you are one of them, you are part of an astonishingly high number. Contrary to some opinions, single parenting is not a problem of ethnic minorities. It spans across all races and ethnicities:

1. One-third of all births among European Americans are to single mothers.

2. In the Hispanic population, 42% of the births are to single mothers.

3. Sixty-nine percent of African American births are to single mothers.[1]

About half of the babies being raised by women

alone are born to unwed mothers, and half are the products of divorce. A 1999 survey indicated that nearly three-quarters of the U.S. population believes that the lack of a father in the home is the most significant family or social problem facing America.[2] So even though the statistics point to great numbers of children living in households without a father present, many of those who responded to the survey must be in that situation themselves.

There can be no doubt that few women would choose to raise a child alone. In most cases, following a divorce or separation, it is the man who leaves the home and family. Judith Wallerstein, an authority on divorce and its harmful effects, states,

"The devastation children feel at divorce or a separation is similar to the feeling when a parent dies unexpectedly, for each experience disrupts close family relationships. Each weakens the protection of the family; each begins with an acute crisis followed by disequilibrium that may last several years or longer, and each introduces a chain of long-lasting changes that are not predictable at the outset."[3]

Studies of families in the United States show

that when there is no father present, children of single mothers have more behavioral problems, poorer academic performance, and lower social skills than children from two-parent families. About 40% of children in father-absent homes have not seen their fathers at all during the past year. Some fathers are in jail, but 26% live in a different state from their children. Half of all children living without a father in the home have never visited their fathers.[4]

The trauma of a father leaving affects the family financially, emotionally, and psychologically, and it also directly affects the children, especially sons. Boys are more frequently and more profoundly affected than girls by their parents' divorce or separation. Many women report their sons' change in behavior after the father leaves. Boys without fathers are less likely to finish high school, more likely to suffer emotionally and economically, and are more likely to have difficulty forming relationships. Studies also suggest that as they develop, boys with absent fathers have a higher likelihood of unemployment, being in jail, and lack of involvement with their own children.

Can a single mother raise a boy to be an emotionally and socially mature adult? Consider your responses to these statements, and then look at the facts that follow.

Perception: *A single mother cannot raise a son satisfactorily.*

Fact: Being a single mother has many challenges, but the challenges are not out of reach. If a woman can give her boy attention, find a male mentor, and provide appropriate discipline with unconditional love, she can raise him alone. Many single mothers have raised productive, morally responsible men because of their dedication to helping their sons reach their potential and refusing to give up despite the challenging circumstances.

Perception: *A mother should be honest with her son about the kind of person the father is.*

Fact: It is common for divorced or abandoned women to talk negatively about their son's father to their sons. Despite the woman's need to vent about the relationship, her comments will probably be destructive to any chance of developing a father-son relationship a boy needs. If a woman needs to unload her feelings about her son's father, she should choose an adult: a minister, parent, friend, or a therapist, but she should not dump her feelings on their son.

The boy doesn't want to hear your personal troubles with his father, and it is beyond his capacity to comprehend this damaged adult relationship. If your son asks where his father is, tell him—even if it is prison. You should assure the boy, however, that he is not responsible for his father's mistakes and that it is all right to be angry or upset or unhappy about his father's situation.

Perception: *Single mothers should not let the son's father visit if there is an ongoing conflict between them.*

Fact: Even though you may have problems with the father, you should not try to keep him from seeing his son. Most sons love their fathers and want to spend time with them. Whatever conflict you have with your son's father, do not let that cause you to shut his father out of his life unless he has abused or tried to harm your son in some way. Boys without paternal involvement tend to display higher rates of physical and verbal aggression, higher rates of substance abuse, and higher school dropout rates than girls living without them. Fathers tend to serve as role models for their sons just as mothers are for their daughters.

Without a father to observe, a boy's ability to become a husband and father himself is hindered because of not viewing male role behavior in his home. A boy without a father figure is like a traveler without a map. He doesn't know how he is going to get to his destination, and in this case, he doesn't really know what that destination is supposed to look like. He may see family relationships in other homes, but that isn't the same. Studies show that boys without fathers more often have marriages that are unhappy, don't communicate well with their spouses, argue more frequently, raise their voice when arguing, and even assault their spouses when they argue.

Perception: *You should wait to communicate with your son's father when your son is in bed or in another room so he won't hear you.*

Fact: Parental conflict only increases your son's anxieties, a problem which can develop into behavioral problems. One young man I counseled had severe difficulty concentrating in class and misbehaved at home, both caused by the anxiety of hearing his parents bickering. At one point, he was so depressed he became suicidal and needed more intensive psychiatric help. He told me many times that he wished his parents would stop fighting. I remember telling his mother not to argue in the house, but she assured me that her son was sleeping or preoccupied with video games. She was surprised when I told her intimate details her son had conveyed to me of a recent argument she and her son's father had when they thought he was sleeping.

Your son will be both upset by your arguing and will unconsciously imitate your method of resolving problems. Don't let children hear adult arguments.

Perception: *A single mother is no more at risk for emotional problems and depression than a mother with a spouse.*

Fact: One study suggested that single mothers are *two times more likely* to experience depression than those who are married. The risk for depression is higher in single mothers because of fewer social supports to help with daily struggles, because of financial hardships and having to work outside of the home. They also tend to have lower self-esteem from sometimes feeling inadequate as a parent. This sort of negative thinking interferes with their ability to interact positively with their sons.

Now that you have a better understanding of some of these beliefs, let's examine the topic of single parenting in more detail. As a woman, you may believe you can be a successful parent or you may feel guilt or frustration. You may be frustrated by problems with your son's father, or you may try to be like a pal to your son to gain his approval. Not giving him the firm direction he needs, however, may backfire because he needs your guidance more than he needs a buddy.

You may also feel guilty because your father was not a part of your life, and you were determined that any children of yours would live with two parents. Negative events typically happen to a woman following divorce: Her income often declines by at least a third. Loss of income often leads to having to move to a smaller home or apartment, and often these are to less expensive and also less desirable neighborhoods. Many low income neighborhoods are in troubled school districts, have higher crime rates, more unsupervised young people and deviant peer groups, and fewer community resources.[5]

You may also feel guilty because your income does not allow you to give your son what his friends or classmates have. If you sacrifice your own needs to give him clothing or money for recreation, you may resent the fact that you have to do without. The expenses of raising a child may also cause you to struggle to pay your bills. You may also have been inconsistent with discipline or allowed your son to get away with things because you wanted him to like you, and now you need to discipline him more firmly because of increased rebellion.

Irrational as it may seem, you may lash out at him because his needs are what push you to overextend yourself. You want him to grow up in a home better than yours and to have more than you had. You know you need help to be a better mother, yet you feel guilty and frustrated. These are all legitimate and universal feelings, but you will need to erase those feelings and learn to think positively about your ability to handle the important task of being your son's mother.

Children are frightened when their parents separate. They are often worried about whether they will have a place to stay and enough to eat. They will typically question: Did I cause my parents to stop loving each other? What did I do wrong?

What is going to happen to me? When these questions occur, a host of mental health problems can emerge. One of these is called an **adjustment disorder**, an unhealthy response to stress such as parental divorce or separation that has lasted less than six months. Common symptoms of an adjustment disorder are episodes of anger, anxiety, sadness, or a combination of these symptoms.

Preschool and early primary grades children may experience what is known as **separation anxiety disorder**. This occurs as a result of the anxiety a child feels when he loses a parent or one of the parents leaves home. This is especially common when a father and mother have recently separated. Many times the young boy may perceive that his mother could also leave him and reacts by becoming irritable and even presenting terribly disruptive displays of anger. Preschoolers may become aggressive and angry towards their mother if they feel the mother is to blame for his father leaving.

Some preschoolers have verbalized their hatred towards their mothers in my office and at times become aggressive. One four-year-old boy slapped and kicked his mother and blamed her for his father not calling and visiting him. She did not respond by disciplining because she felt guilty about the situation. Anxiety among preschoolers is also high because of the nature of their reasoning ability. Preschoolers struggle to tell the difference between what is real and what is fantasy and may have fantasies about the family living together again.

A child will typically respond to parental separation by either internalizing or externalizing his problems. Internalized problems do not cause much of a disturbance to others but are manifested by withdrawing socially, having difficulty sleeping, experiencing depression, or suffering from anxiety. Externalized problems are usually disruptive or harmful to others and may include angry outbursts and physical aggression.

Other common problems of parental separation are the child completely denying the existence of the problem or taking on the task of parental responsibilities by offering to get a job to help pay bills. Many preteens and adolescents may "act out" their feelings in uncharacteristic ways such as an increase in rebellion, foul language, aggression or all three. Typically, frequent instances of defiance, aggression, and noncompliant behaviors predict not only problems in school for younger boys but potentially serious health and behavioral problems in adolescence. Drug abuse, depression, juvenile delinquency, and dropping out of school are but a few.

Our society currently faces an epidemic of youth violence, and much of it can be traced to boys growing up without fathers. Many violent, anti-social young males have grown up neglected, emotionally abused, and rejected by their fathers. They lack a father who is a positive role model and have not been guided by a man through the process of becoming a man.

The importance of a nurturing, loving family in preventing violent behavior has been well documented. A 1988 study by the U.S. Department of Justice showed that more than half of the juveniles in detention facilities had come from single families, and three out of four teenagers in the general population were not living in two-parent families. In a survey of research on the issue, Bryce J. Christensen flatly concluded, "The broken home produces many of the nation's most violent criminals." [6]

Educators have long observed the trend among young men to unrealistically aspire to become professional athletes and entertainers instead of preparing for professions that require scholarship. Many males view athletes and entertainers as living the good life with the finances to do what they want. How often have you heard a newly signed rookie say the first thing he is going to do with his signing bonus is to buy his mother a house. He may have been the product of a home without an adult male and is painfully aware of the struggles the family went through without the financial support of a father. He can now be the man and provide for his mother who struggled to take care of him.

When an intact family has meals and spends time together, the children have a much greater chance of growing up feeling a part of something that supports them, but many families don't operate that way. If a son does not feel a part of something positive that supports him, he will look for love elsewhere and explore other avenues for attention.

Often these alternatives lead him to do things such as steal, fight, or engage in other illegal and dangerous activities just to be a *part* of something. In the initiation rituals of some of the notorious street gangs, a person must endure violent beatings to become a member. Those who survive, though, have a "family" for life, so they accept the torture and pain.

Families today experience pressures that didn't exist in the last century, but with these new problems come new ways to handle them. Chapter 2 will examine your parenting style and show you how to get on the path to being a better parent.

2

PARENTING PRACTICES

All parents discuss their children with other
parents. They compare how their children behave
in certain circumstances, what problems they are
having with them, and what they have tried—successfully and unsuccessfully--to change their child's
negative behaviors. Single mothers are no different,
but they don't have a male to take on some of the
burden of parenting and discipline. They know their
son needs a male in the home, but since there is not
one, they have to rely on their own resources and the
example of their own parents.

Every parent employs a particular parenting
style, even if they don't realize it and couldn't
name or describe it. Regardless of marital status,
if you are reading this book to learn how to help

yourself, this chapter will help you to see what your style is and whether it is the best one for you to use.

Psychologist Diana Baumrind studied various parenting styles many years ago based on her observations.[7] Based on her findings, she established four basic styles of parenting she believes most parents directly or indirectly use: authoritarian, permissive, uninvolved, and authoritative.

This chapter illustrates and examines the different parenting styles and shows how each style influences your parenting with your sons. The following are various scenarios that look at different parenting styles used by different parents.

The first parenting style is the *authoritarian* way of parenting. Authoritarian parents tend to be very controlling, punitive, callous, and cold hearted when believing their sons have done something inappropriate. It can be as severe as withholding all of their son's privileges for earning a low grade in a subject. I knew a mother who had punished her son for two months for one failing grade, despite earning average to above average grades on the rest of his report card. All parents want their children to do well, but punishing a child for two months for a failing grade is extreme.

Authoritarian parents virtually do not give a child room to breathe or make mistakes. Whatever they say is set in stone, and there is no room for discussion. This type of parent will not tolerate any sort of disagreement or entertain negotiation. The child is constantly demanded to do what he is told without question, do housework, and earn good grades. All of us have known parents who try to rear their children like this. An interesting fact about this parenting style is that many single mothers who suffer from depression are authoritarian. This type of parenting style contradicts a parent's thinking because instead of children responding positively to the parent's demands, they tend to become more withdrawn, have lower self-esteem, and lack social skills. At the same time, the most *permissive* parents are also those who often suffer from depression, a phenomenon that will be discussed further in this chapter.

What are the direct effects of an authoritarian parent on a boy? Boys reared in an authoritarian household are frequently rebellious, hostile, and angry because their lives are tightly controlled. Two boys I grew up with who came from an authoritarian household were punished by being forced to do rigorous workouts as consequences for their actions. They were required to rise early in the morning and run several miles, followed by pushups and sit-ups to the point of exhaustion before school. Consequently, as they developed into teenagers they became quite rebellious in school and in the community and refused to take directions from any authority. They also had problems with the legal system as young adults. Essentially, their authoritarian parents caused them to rebel against any authority and break the law due to their harsh parenting style.

To illustrate, let's examine the authoritarian style of Mary and how she may respond to her son Tom, a typical 14-year-old who is beginning to develop strong peer relationships and wants to spend more time with his friends. He asks his mother if he can spend the weekend with a 16-year-old friend from high school. Mary will not give permission because she has not met Tom's parents and knows little about his family.

The authoritarian

The conversation might go something like this.

"Mom, Fred invited me to spend the weekend

at his house to play video games and other
stuff. Can I?"

"Are you kidding me? No way!" replied Mary.

"What do you mean? That's not fair!"

"I said you're not going over to his house, and
that's it!" replied Mary.

"Why?" demanded Tom.

"Because I said so, and I will absolutely not
negotiate with a teenager!"

Tom became very angry, and he had every
reason to be. His mother could have told him her
reasons, and although he might have continued
to argue with her, at least she would have granted
him the courtesy of being told why. A boy that
age is not a child. She had good reasons, but her
refusal to discuss it enraged Tom and strained the
relationship further. This approach, as you can
see, is hurtful to your son.

The permissive parent

Permissive mothers tend to exert almost no
control. They offer quite a bit of warmth, which
is important, as it shows they love the child, but
they do not set guidelines or limits for their child
and let him do as he wishes. This degree of per-
missiveness communicates to the child that his

mother does not care what he does and therefore cares little about him.

Here is a scenario with another 14-year-old, by the name of David and his mother:

"Mom, Fred invited me to spend the weekend at his house to play video games and other stuff. Can I?"

"Sure. Have fun."

His mother may be trying to tell him that she trusts him, but she doesn't question anything about what he is going to be doing. David might well feel she is not interested in him. He might be a good boy, but good boys need attention from their parents, too. Consequently as a result of this parenting style, David may not develop adequate social skills if his mother does not talk with him about his daily activities or may eventually fail to develop self-control if he does not have any guidelines or rules to abide by. His mother wants to be a friend and let her son enjoy life, but she should have asked him more about going to his friend's house: if adults were going to be present, what time he would return, and other details.

If a mother or other parent is always permissive, then when someone *does* exert control such as a teacher or coach, the boy may become frustrated and angry because he is not accustomed to rules. Children need discipline and to have their limits set upon them to feel loved and to learn to understand the reason for rules and respecting authority.

Being uninvolved

Uninvolved mothers provide neither *warmth nor control*. They are detached emotionally and see their role as being simply a provider of physical needs. A typical conversation could go something like this between the son of an uninvolved mother and his friend.

"Hey, thanks for inviting me for the weekend. Did your mother say it was OK?"

"No, I didn't even ask her 'cause she lets me do whatever I want. I don't think what I do matters to her."

This boy may develop a host of mental health issues. If he feels his mother doesn't seem to care what he does, then who will? Some mothers never utter the comforting words "I love you" to their sons. These boys tell me that no one cares about them, and to get some attention—even negative attention—they will disrupt classes in school and are unruly in the neighborhood so their mothers will have to notice them. As a result they receive negative attention from their mothers or recognition for anti-social acts from their peers. Boys need abundant love from their mothers, especially when they do not have a father in the house. It is an unfortunate myth that boys are not emotional and do not need as much love as daughters. Imagine how alone a young boy must feel if he has been rejected by his father and is living with a mother who treats him with indifference.

Exerting authority (authoritative)

Parents who exert their rightful authority and are firm in giving directions and setting consistent guidelines or limits are those who behave like parents should behave. These parents reason with their children and explain their decisions. They neither smother the child with restrictions and excessive rules nor do they let them do anything they wish. This balance tends to foster independence in children. Remember the previous scenario with Tom and his mother? In that scenario, Tom's mother used an authoritarian parenting style. Here is an example of Tom's mother using an authoritative parenting style.

"Mom, Fred invited me to spend the weekend

at his house to play video games and other stuff. Can I?"

"Who is going to be in the house with you and Fred over the weekend?"

"His 18-year-old brother will be there."

"Tom, I don't know Fred's family, and I don't think it's a good idea."

"Why? We won't do anything wrong."

"I know you won't, but here's a compromise. You can go over on Saturday as long as you're home by dinnertime. I want to meet his parents before you spend the night. Maybe after that you can stay over the weekend."

This scenario explained to Tom his mother's reasons and offered a compromise they could both live with. Boys whose parents treat them this way are far more likely to be friendly, assertive, and cooperative. They are more successful, likeable, better able to regulate their behaviors, and are normally higher achievers, and learn that there should be give and take in any relationship. Any parent can learn how to become an effective authoritative parent; it just takes practice.

I am sure you can see that the most effective parenting is an authoritative style which includes reasoning, giving a rationale for your decisions, and cultivating a warm, loving environment. After reading this chapter, you may conclude that your parenting style may not be authoritative enough and that you want to change it. If so, the next few chapters will illustrate how you can become this type of loving and emotionally supportive parent.

3

PRUDENT PARENTING

"Sam, why are you always so bad? It's because of you I have high blood pressure that could kill me. If it weren't for you, I wouldn't have to work so hard to clean up behind you and get you to do your homework or worry so much. If you loved me, you wouldn't act this way."

This scenario goes on day in and day out throughout many households throughout the world. This particular mother doesn't really believe these things, but she has gotten tired of yelling and nagging, so she has resorted to blaming and criticizing to make her child feel as guilty as she can. Imagine how this boy would feel if his mother *did* die from a stroke caused by high blood pressure. He would undoubtedly suffer from guilt the rest of his life.

This style of communication is very damaging because Sam's mother is basically saying that her son's behavior dictates whether she loves him or not. This is called *conditional love* which means you base your love for your son on his behavior. This kind of attempt at manipulation does not work, however, and it will surely harm the relationship. Many parents use this mechanism of communication as a means of discipline. Consider the situation a mother could potentially create. The son already feels rejected by his absent father, and now his mother is basically rejecting him, too.

This manipulation technique will only increase his levels of anxiety and possibly create depression and eventual anger in him. Why? Because he is going to believe that it is not possible to please his mother, and that he may even be the cause of his father's absence in his life. That is an enormous burden for a child to carry, and it is terribly unfair to make him feel responsible in any way for the family's situation.

Thus, the preceding scenario sets the stage for this important chapter on learning effective communication. The title of this chapter, "Prudent

Parenting," essentially means dealing with your child wisely. One of the most important concepts about prudent parenting is knowing how to communicate the words and actions you should and should *not* use with your son.

Here is an easy way to help you to remember the communication behaviors to avoid if at all possible when communicating to your son.

It's **BOY: B** is for **blaming, O** is for **ordering**, and **Y** is for **yelling** (or preaching or lecturing too much or too loudly). This should be easy to remember.

<u>Blaming</u>: Sam's mother blamed him, contending he did not love her because he continued to misbehave which, in turn, caused her hypertension (high blood pressure). As a single mother, life may be stressful, but making negative, blaming comments will make the situation much worse for you and for your son. One result is that he may give up trying to please you and not try to improve his behavior at all because he believes it is impossible and you will continue to put him down. Likewise, he may develop low self-esteem because you blame him for your poor health, and you measure his love for you by his behavior.

Another damaging aspect of blaming is to compare your son with another child who is succeeding. Comparisons will always set up resentment and hostility. Boys are not miniature men, and there will be days in which his actions *will* cause your blood pressure to rise. No matter what he does, though, never measure his love for you by his behavior, and never blame him for something he has not caused.

Ordering This is what a parent does who tells the child what to do, when to do it, and allows for no negotiating. Sometimes there should not be negotiation, but some negotiation is helpful in the development of your child's sense of responsibility and boundaries. Negotiation helps him to become responsible for his actions and helps him to become effective at communicating his desires. In essence, negotiation will improve your son's social skills, which will help him in school and in the future. Being able to work out compromises will also give him the sense that he has some rights in the household.

Yelling: This is a problem that many parents struggle with. Yelling stems from frustration. This is tougher to deal with than the others. If your child gets into trouble at school and you get that dreaded phone call, your first reaction may be to launch into a tirade about what he has done wrong. While it is important to talk with him about the consequences of poor choices, it is not necessary to lecture, yell, blame, and scold at length each time your son gets into trouble. You may even be tempted to compare his actions to his father's behavior, but telling him he is just like his father when he does something wrong can become a handy crutch you use any time he misbehaves. It dumps all of the bad things he has been told about his father right onto his shoulders, and that is not where that guilt should rest.

I cannot stress strongly enough that you should **never tell him he is like his father** when he misbehaves. Ironically, he may *want to be like the father* he wishes he had a relationship with and would probably try to please him to gain that relationship—even if it was by some illegal or immoral means. In other ways, though, *he knows how much pain* his father may have inflicted on the family and his mother, and he probably tells himself he will never be a father like that. The conflicting emotions from being compared with his father can cause untold harm to a boy who is struggling to grow up.

Yelling will also cause your son to eventually just tune you out and not even hear your words because it is the same lecture all over again. Secondly, yelling teaches your son that it is acceptable to yell when communicating with you and others. When yelling is really called for, such as in an emergency, he may not know that it is serious.

So how do you become an effective communicator? For one, you should listen attentively to what your son has to say and attempt to understand his feelings. One good practice is to clarify with him that you know what he means by restating in your words what he has said. That will let him know how you heard it. A good time for learning how to communicate better is spending time talking with him as often as you can. It could be during a trip to a ball game, going to the park, visiting a neighbor, or even watching television. During these times, you need for him to know that he has your primary attention.

Younger boys need more time than older ones. An older boy will become busier and more involved in social and outside activities, but you should still be available for him when he needs your support or wants to spend time with you.

What if you are not used to talking with your son calmly because of a strained relationship or are wondering how to build and strengthen your relationship with him? Here are some phrases you can use to begin a discussion.

> "Tell me something good that happened at school today."
>
> "I know you like basketball. How do you learn how to dribble without looking at the ball?"
>
> "Let's count how many stars we see through our telescopes tonight."
>
> "This weekend is going to be sunny and warm. Do you want to do something with me tomorrow?"

The way you talk will model for your sons the way *they* should talk. Look at him when you talk to him and keep your voice at a moderate level. Be aware of your facial expressions. Some mothers have a frustrated, bothered look on their faces when they are communicating with their sons in counseling, and I imagine it is the same look they have with them at home. You should be aware if you are tense, as that will be reflected in your face.

Try to soften your expression, and your tone of voice should soften as well.

Answer him with "Tell me more about what happened" or "Oh, that's wonderful that you pulled up your algebra grade." This sort of communication will not only help decrease your stress but your son's also. These responses will also help to validate your son's positive feelings about himself. Remember that you are really having to do the work of two supportive parents, so whatever you do is twice as important as it would be if you had a partner to share in the raising of your son.

Another essential component to communicating effectively to your son is using what mental health professionals call "I-messages." These are statements that allow you to express your feelings honestly and respectfully. Here is an example. Your son physically attacked his sibling over a disagreement over a video game, which led to an argument. So using an I-message, you would say, "You know, Brent, I feel worried when you hit your brother because you know you can hurt him. The "when" part allows you to tell your son in a non-blaming way about his problem behavior.

I-messages identify your child's inappropriate

behavior and communicate to him that *you* know *he already knows the rules*. That puts the responsibility on him for the choices he makes. The important thing is to focus on the **i**nappropriate behavior rather than on the child. Instead of saying, "Why do you make me so mad!" after he talks back to you, it would be better to say, "I feel very angry when you talk back to me," focusing on the behavior of talking back rather than your son who is doing it.

Parents tend to become very concerned with children's grades. So what is wrong with asking, "Why are you such a terrible student?" The reason is simple: It is confrontational and invites resentment and argument. Remember "You" messages push people away, and "I" messages pull them in. If you start into a conversation on a poor grade report this way, then there is an excellent chance that your son will become defensive and argumentative which will lead to conflict. And seriously, what reasonable answer can he give?

"Because I don't study." (A parent should know this.)

"My teachers hate me." (an ancient excuse and almost always false)

"I don't understand what we're reading." (a strong possibility)

"You don't help me with my homework."

(Throw the blame back at the mother.)

And the list has no end. The point is that you should probably never ask your child a question if you don't already have a pretty good idea of the answer. You know if he hangs out on the street after school instead of coming home to study, so why not address *that* issue? You know he talks with his friends or girlfriend for hours on the phone, so why not *restrict that privilege*? You know he watches television for hours every evening, so why not put a stop to that until his grades improve?

Imagine your employer coming in to your office and saying to you, "I'm pleased that you've improved your productivity. Here are some more things I want you to try to improve even more." The scene is private, and the message encouraging. But what if he or she approached you in the hallway with other employees around and said, "You're just not getting the work done. When are you going to learn how to work more efficiently?" This latter setting suggests both spontaneous anger and a lack of respect for you, the employee. And what possible answer can you give to the question? "I'll work faster when you get off my back," or "If you didn't unload so much work on me, I might be able to finish something." Wouldn't you be inclined to give a smart answer back to save face in front of co-workers? Wouldn't your son give the same kind of sarcastic answer?

The words communicate the same information, but the effects on you would be far different. In the first scenario, you would be eager to try new methods to improve your work, and you would also feel the boss believes you are capable of doing better. In the second case, though, your focus would be on your embarrassment and your anger with the boss. With others listening, you might feel he is setting you up to be fired.

The parallel with your son:

Situation 1: Mom loves me and thinks I can do better. She's going to help me so I can improve.

Situation 2: Mom doesn't care how I feel. She embarrasses me in front of the neighbors, and I'm ashamed to talk to any of them now. She'd probably like it if I ran away.

So try these **I**-messages and remember to think of how your son feels when you use a "you" message to talk to him. This could be a good reason you and your son may have a contentious relationship or why he seems to tune you out when you try to talk to him, causing you even more frustration.

Here are some suggestions for using I-messages with your son.

Look at him when you talk to him. Some mothers do not make eye contact with their sons when they talk to them and talk to me about the boy as if he were not even in the room. You know how that makes you feel: like an *object* which is the subject of discussion rather than someone worthy of consideration. When you look into your son's eyes and communicate with an I-message, it tells him you are serious about what you are saying.

Let your facial expression reflect your message. If you have a half smile on your face when you are making a serious request, it tells him you are not serious. Your son may think you are joking with him, and that is not what you want to communicate.

Keep a calm tone of voice, and keep your body language under control. Many parents often lose their cool when talking to their children. When you are calm and can communicate in a calm manner your son will observe that you are in control.

When you scream and lose control it communicates that you have lost control and directly gives your son the control and sends the message that it is okay to communicate in that manner when communicating. Remember that your children observe the way you behave and communicate since you are probably the most important adult figure in their lives.

4

BUILDING SELF-ESTEEM

Self-esteem is a term heard a lot these days, and it can be interpreted in both negative and positive ways. People with low self-esteem don't think they are worth very much, while those with a sense of high self-esteem believe they have value as human beings. All children need a sense of belonging to or being a part of something, and if they cannot obtain it from a positive source like home or school, they will seek it in places mothers would rather they did not go: in gangs, on the street, or in illegal activities.

In a perfect family, all children and family members will feel a part of a whole, but sometimes the family structure is fragile. When the male or father is absent from the family and the mother has all of the responsibilities for raising the family, taking care of the household, earning a living, she can become impatient—and it is understandable why she would. You may struggle with low self-esteem of your own, due to the stressors of your role. The purpose of this chapter, then, is to learn how to be positive and foster healthy self-esteem in your son. Your son thrives on hearing you compliment him just as much as you enjoy hearing compliments from others. The following are examples of ways you can hurt your son's self-esteem.

Don't compare him unfavorably with neighbors or relatives: "Why *aren't you as smart as your cousin Oscar? He is on the honor roll. I guess you're just the dumb one in the family.*"

Don't pick out the negative in what he does. Instead of telling him you appreciate it when you don't have to ask him to take out the trash, the negative parent would say, *"It's about time you finally did something right."*

Don't label him in ways that stay in his mind. *"Stop bothering me, Jonathan. You're just a pest."*

Don't over-generalize or make "absolute" statements: *"You* never *think before you act."* *"You* always *speak before you think.* Adolescent boys have especially fragile self-esteem due to their rapid developmental and hormonal changes. Although girls attempt suicide more frequently, the rate of suicide is higher for boys than girls. Depression, striving to be perfect, and a high level of stress and anxiety are related to a greater risk of suicide. This is not to say your son will commit suicide; however, your sons will believe you when you tell them something about the way they look or criticize their behavior or their intelligence.

A handsome boy may eventually believe it if you tell him he is ugly. A considerate young man will think he is selfish if he hears it often enough. They might all eventually believe whatever you tell him--whether it's negative OR positive. The way they think they are or see themselves because of what they are told will become truth to them.

Thus, it is very important to encourage your son to see himself positively. The following gives you examples of ways you can help to foster positive self-esteem in your son.

Pay attention to what he is doing and let him know you are proud of the good things he does— whether large or small. It may be as simple as helping without being asked, or it may be something really important like improving his grades. The important thing is for him to know you both notice and appreciate his accomplishments. If he brings home a good grade on a math test, and his grades had once been failing, praise him. Don't make the mistake that so many parents do and tell your son you expect the next grade to be better. That belittles his accomplishment and makes him feel like there is **nothing** he can do to please you. It could be a piece of artwork that he has been working on which he is really proud of. Even if it isn't the kind of art you like, praise him for finishing it, and post it where others can see it—if he wants you to.

After I encouraged a mother to praise her son more, I watched one mother tell her son that she was going to hang his perfect attendance award on the refrigerator when they got home after our counseling session. He became so proud and excited he could not stop smiling. He was so happy and proud that his mother appreciated his efforts to attend school regularly and thought so highly of his award that she would display it on the refrigerator for everyone to view.

If your son participates in sports, you should go

to his games and cheer for him when he is intro-
duced or when he scores a point or gets a hit. It
will be exhilarating for him to see his mother with
the other spectators applauding him for scor-
ing a goal or in the audience when he is given an
award. Your support will encourage him to work
even harder at what he is doing and *will improve*
his self-esteem.

Thus, consistently give your son a large amount of
praise and support when he does something well or
something that pleases you. Parents should be aware
of what their children are doing. If your child is doing well, you should let him know you noticed.

**Look for opportunities to tell him what he is
doing well**. Children know their parents are on
the lookout for things they do *wrong*, so let them
know that you also notice the good things. If he
is sharing well with peers or siblings, washing
the dishes without being asked, asking if he can
watch television after completing his homework,
and taking turns with siblings over choosing the
programs to watch, he is acting positively and doing what you want him to do. All of these are all
examples of opportunities for noting his positive
behavior. Praising him encourages him to think

positively about himself and at the same time elevates his self-esteem. If he gets the little rewards like praise or a hug, he will continue to do those things that bring on the rewards.

Think about how you feel when your employer tells you how much he appreciates the work you do and that it really contributes positively to the company efficiency or image. If your neighbor compliments you on the way you keep up your yard or on the talent you have with houseplants or any other thing that gives you recognition, it makes you happy. It gives you a sense of self-worth and boosts your self-esteem. Your son thrives on the same kinds of good words you do.

If your supervisor only notices you when you do something wrong, or if your evaluations note only areas you should improve in, it does not make you feel good about yourself. You don't have much drive to do better because what you do well has not been noticed. On the other hand, if you are praised along with the suggestions for improvement, you want to do whatever it takes to live up to that praise. Children respond the same way as adults to this treatment. Remember, though, that lavish praise one does not deserve is not productive. Your son knows when he deserves praise and when he does not, and if you brag on him all the time, he will begin to believe that you are being insincere, and it will not have the intended effect. In fact, it might make him feel like he is doing better than he actually is. Honesty with him is the essential ingredient. Praise when he has earned praise, and scold when he does wrong.

Many mothers criticize and blame their children for every little thing that they do wrong. This can become a habit, and if you are guilty of this, you may not be aware of it. Your constant criticism and negativity damages your son's self-esteem. This feeling that he is never good enough can cause serious behavioral problems and academic difficulties that will affect him negatively. He may develop the idea that whatever he does his mother will find fault with him, and since he can never seem to do anything right in her eyes, he might as well stop trying. A young adult male I counseled a few years ago had developed severe self-esteem and confidence problems because his mother constantly criticized him throughout his childhood. He came to me seeking help as an adult because of his intense sense of inadequacy which affected all areas of his life.

The feeling that a boy can never do anything well enough to please a parent can cause a reaction that leads to a full-blown rebellion. You never want this to happen, but demanding perfection can become a habit and lead to your seeming to be impossible to please. Many mothers criticize their sons in my office, and the humiliation on the faces of these boys is heartbreaking. Those who criticize their sons incessantly have sons who have much lower self-esteem than those whose mothers are less critical.

The last point to remember about fostering healthy self-esteem in your son is to teach him how to say positive *self-statements* to himself when he is frustrated or sad. Positive self-statements are words or phrases that make people feel better about themselves and their lives when things are not going well for them. These statements not only foster healthy self-esteem, but help to strengthen a person's ability to handle the challenges of life. Reframing negative thinking is a tool anyone can use to help in facing the challenges of life.

Here are some examples: Your son is having a

lot of trouble learning algebra or Spanish. You can suggest that he think of and use phrases such as "I can do it" or "If you believe it, you can achieve it" Phrases such as these can help your son believe in himself. Many books have inspirational phrases you can teach your son to use to foster a healthy self-esteem. Remember that if your son feels positive about himself it will produce positive results for your life and your son's.

5

ESTABLISHING BOUNDARIES

W hat are boundaries, and how do they apply in a family between a mother and son? Boundaries are the limitations you establish so that he knows the clear differences between what is appropriate *(what he is allowed to do)* and what is not *(behaviors you will not accept).* Many parents seem unaware of how to identify and establish appropriate boundaries, and because of that, their relationship with their sons has gotten out of control or has created complex problems. That is the reason it is such an important issue to address in the pages of this book. This chapter presents some of the most frequently asked questions from single mothers about boundaries throughout my years as a professional. The first question is a bit tricky, for it involves behavior that might be appropriate when your son is young but becomes inappropriate as he enters preadolescence.

Question: "Should I allow my son to sleep with me in my bed regularly? He is often frightened and comes into my bedroom during the night and needs to be comforted."

Answer: This, without question, is the most controversial and serious boundary issue I have ever had to deal with. It seems so innocent on the face of it, but it can have really destructive results. I have known of boys as old as twelve who are still allowed to sleep in the bed with their mothers regularly, and I know this is absolutely detrimental to both the mother and to her son. You may believe that allowing him to sleep with you regularly is a loving thing to do and that it will help him to feel greater security and a sense of attachment. You may also feel more secure yourself because you are sharing your space with your child. On the contrary, however, as comfortable as it may seem at the time, it will probably create a situation that is both unhealthy and counter-productive.

If your son sleeps with you regularly in your

bed, he will begin to feel that he is equal to an adult and will develop the notion that he is the man of the house as his father was. In his mind he is on a level similar to yours, and he may begin to think that he has the same authority you have. This situation will make disciplining him much more difficult.

Your son may also become more dependent upon you and need the security that sleeping in your bed gives him. This may create difficulty in his being able to develop independence. Consider what will happen when you decide he should start sleeping in his own bed. You can be sure there will be a serious conflict.

When he reaches puberty, he will experience many physical and emotional changes and may develop guilt and anxiety when these changes occur. He is sleeping in the bed with his mother, who is a woman, and he is bound to suffer conflicts in his thinking when he learns the facts of life, experiences puberty and all that goes along with these changes.

A mother and son sleeping in the same bed on a regular basis is a bad idea even if there are space limitations where you live. If there is not a room where he can have his own bed, you should find a way to make a bed for him on the sofa, or get a portable mattress or cot, or figure out some other way for him to sleep without sharing your bed. Sleeping with you regularly is simply a bad idea that will inevitably create difficulties for you and for him at some point in your relationship.

Question: "Should I make my son feel that he is the 'man of the house' so he will feel a greater sense of responsibility for what goes on and can take some of the responsibilities off of me?"

Answer: Many single mothers make the mistake of giving this responsibility to their sons because they want to make their sons feel like they are an important part of the household. This is **always** a big mistake. It is a mistake because your son will take your statement literally and begin to treat you as if he is your equal and try to make decisions that **you** should be making. He will begin to feel he is entitled to special treatment, and he will treat you as his subordinate. I recently met with a single mother who made this mistake and is regretting it dearly. Her adolescent son tells her when to turn off the television and when to go to bed. He is also draining her limited income because he feels that he is entitled to make financial decisions of all kinds. He demands money from her so he can buy clothes and video games, and she gives in to his every demand. This is a relationship out of control and an example of one mother who mistakenly empowered her son.

Another statement I heard from a mother was "Dr. Passley, we won't be able to keep our appointment today because my son said his favorite television show conflicts with the appointment, and he'll be upset with me if he misses his show." Or "I'll have to ask to my son if he wants to go to church tomorrow. He's going out with friends tonight and may come in late. He'll probably be angry with me if I wake him up too early." You are the parent, and your son is the child--no matter how old he is. It is your responsibility to take control of what is going on in your house. In the next chapter I will show you how.

Question: "Should my son and I use our only bathroom at the same time? We live in a small apartment, and with one bathroom, and being so busy in the mornings, a lot of times we don't have time to wait until the other has finished."

Answer: You probably know the answer to this,

but you want someone to spell it out for you. As a boy develops emotionally and physically, it is inappropriate for mother and son to bathe or use the toilet with the other one present. An easy solution to the problem is for one of you to get up earlier so that the bathroom is free when the other one is ready to use it. This could be based on who needs to leave earlier for school or work, or you could even alternate weeks so that neither has to get up earlier all the time.

You should both have privacy when you are attending to these personal needs regardless of your limited space. One mother reported to me that her 7-year-old son asked questions about her body when she was taking a shower and wondered if that was appropriate. She said she wanted him to have an open, communicative relationship with her and doesn't want to stifle his curiosity. My response is that you *should* have an open relationship with your son, but he should not watch you when you are bathing.

Question: "Is it appropriate for me to search my son's room if I suspect that he is doing something illegal or is engaged in activities which could harm him in any way? What is the difference between invading his privacy and doing what any mother would do if she suspected his behavior might potentially hurt him?"

Answer: This can be a seriously conflicting issue between all parents and children, and it is one that requires a delicate balance between respecting the young child's personal space and privacy and your being sure that he is not engaged in dangerous or illegal activity. As a professional who has studied these issues, I believe you have the right to check your son's belongings if you are suspicious of his activities or note some warning signs. Here are some signs to look for:

1. There is a negative change in your son's behavior or moods.

2. He is hanging out with different kinds of friends from the ones you used to know.

3. His grades are dropping.

4. He is becoming more secretive about his possessions and doesn't like to answer questions about where he is going and who he will be with.

5. He has lost interest in hobbies and/or sports that used to be important to him.

6. You notice unusual fragrances on his clothing or in his room. Even pleasant fragranc-

es—if they are unfamiliar—may indicate an attempt to mask the odor of some drugs.

7. You notice a change in his sleeping and eating habits.

8. He is borrowing more money than usual from you and you notice you have unaccounted for cash.

9. You notice physical changes such as needle marks, bruises, red eyes and persistent coughing.

You have the right–in fact, the obligation-- to know what is happening in your son's life. A survey taken nearly six years ago of approximately 50,000 American students showed that almost 40% of high school seniors and more than a third of 8th graders report having used marijuana within the past year.[8] Additionally, the majority of high school seniors admit to having had an alcoholic beverage within the past month.[8] These statistics do not mean your son is engaging in any kind of drug use. They do mean that if you suspect he is, the statistics suggest a strong likelihood that he might be.

With so many pressures your son encounters in this new century, it is imperative that you go with your intuition and check his room for anything that looks suspicious. This also goes for the use of the Internet. According to the Kaiser Family Foundation,[9] twice as many children have computers in their bedroom than just five years ago. Many youths use chat rooms on the Internet to meet friends and socialize.

Such Internet sites as www.myspace.com have received a lot of media attention for unsavory things which have been connected to them. According to the site, 22% of its users are registered as under 18, but since there is no way for the site to check, much older people are likely trolling for innocent youth to seduce. In recent months, there have been cases of sexual attacks, gang fights, and other dangerous activities associated with these sites. It is easy for a young person to become drawn into their culture, and parents have to be on the alert. The popular news program *Dateline* ran a series called "To Catch a Predator" which showed how criminals use the Internet to contact and then meet underage youth for sexual encounters. As modern technology becomes more sophisticated, these types of problems will likely increase.

One suggestion for controlling Internet access is

to put your son's computer in a place that allows you to see the monitor. A boy will be tempted to view pornography, a practice which can cause a host of problems for his young, developing mind. If he knows you can see what he is viewing, he is far less likely to search for images he knows he should not be viewing and which you can observe.

There are some basic guidelines for computer use to protect your family.

Parents should teach their sons to do the following:

1. Think before you click: Who are you e-mailing or chatting with? What are you saying, and how are you saying it? What do you know about this person?

2. Do not share private or demographic information with anyone you meet online.

3. Do not do or say anything online that you know you shouldn't do in real life.

Parents should do these to protect their computers:

1. Install anti-virus software and update it regularly.

2. Install spyware-blocking software and programs that filter out spam and phishing

schemes on your computer. Much of this is available as freeware or is offered by Internet service providers.

3. Never open an attachment from someone you do not know and inform your son of this also.

If you find something you are unsure about in his room or on the Internet, you should talk to him frankly and try to stop him from making wrong choices which could lead to serious consequences for him. If you are **sure** he is using illegal substances or alcohol, you should seek professional help before his problem becomes something even more serious.

Question: "Is it okay for grandparents or a babysitter to discipline my son? Isn't that crossing the line or violating boundaries? Shouldn't the parent be the only disciplinarian in a child's life?"

Answer: If you mean inflicting physical punishment, then, no, it is not acceptable for anyone to do that to your son. If you mean another person correcting him if he misbehaves or withholding privileges when he is in that person's care, then, yes, that should be allowed. It is important for children to have other adults in their lives who can provide direction to them.

Although there is nothing wrong with allowing discipline to be carried out by a caretaker, there is a problem if that person does not enforce your rules. If you tell your son's grandmother that you do not want him to be allowed to do something because he disobeyed you the previous day, she should honor your directions and enforce your rule. If she disregards your consequences and believes the punishment is unfair and grants him the privilege, it will minimize your authority and create a potential conflict among the three of you.

Anyone who takes care of your son for you should know and follow your rules of discipline so he will be treated with consistency across all settings. Consistent discipline, boundaries, and love will benefit both of you now and in the long run.

6

DEDICATED DISCIPLINE

What is *dedicated* discipline, and how is it different from just "discipline?" Read on.

"My son Lucas is often disrespectful to adults, and that is so embarrassing, but he is even more unpleasant to me! I am his mother, and I love him. I just don't understand why he treats me this way after I have provided so much for him," says the single mother of a challenging 10-year-old.

This illustration may be hard to imagine or envision for a person who does not have children or who has a husband or male in the household to help in the task of parenting. A woman without a son may wonder how or why a mother would tolerate this behavior. What could cause a 10-year-old boy to deliberately create embarrassing scenes with his mother when others were present? This mother is missing the point: if respect is not demanded at home, it is highly unlikely that Lucas will either show her respect or respect other adults.

Often single mothers have no one to support them when a son rebels against their parenting. It is much easier to discipline boys if there is a male in the household because men are usually bigger and stronger, and a man may be less likely to become emotionally upset when he is hurt. If the mother cries or otherwise shows that she is really upset, the son may see this as weakness and desperation and recognize that he has the upper hand with his weaker mother.

Single parenting is a challenging task, no matter how experienced a parent may be. Combining the roles of job and parenthood are challenging enough for a two-parent family; however, if you have to do it alone, the difficulties are multiplied.

There is a certain misconception among many adults that children should be compliant and listen to them without any resistance. Their thinking is that if a child argues that he is disobedient. Contrary to this notion, children are very different from the miniature adults they may appear to be. They have their own ideas and will test their limits to see how far they can go. This is particularly true with boys. Although they don't have the maturity of an adult, they are probably smarter than you may believe.

If you have repeatedly and predictably given in to your son's demands and threats of destructive behavior—or if he has actually been destructive—he knows how to get what he wants and can often think quickly enough to manipulate you into giving in again. After awhile he may simply do what he wants without bothering to ask you.

Every child has a different temperament, and each one presents different challenges. However, you absolutely have to provide both consistent love and discipline to teach your son to have respect for authority and to foster in him the development of strong, positive values. Here is an important key to remember about parenting: *The more parental control you exercise early in your son's development, the less conflict you and he will have as he grows older and develops into a man.*

Child discipline is paramount in producing a responsible boy and successful man. Do the following occur frequently in your interactions with your son?

1. You yell at him.

2. You are reluctant to discipline him in public because you fear what his reaction might be.

3. You feel overwhelmed by his behavior and feel you may not like him as much as you once did.

4. You fear upsetting him because he can be so unpleasant.

5. You hesitate to threaten or carry out punishment for fear of his retaliation.

6. You give in and do his chores for him after you have already told him to do them numerous times.

7. You make excuses for his inappropriate behaviors.

8. You don't want to be out in public or at a social occasion with him because you fear he will embarrass you.

Spiritual values are paramount to a child's developing a sense of self-worth and connection to God. The Book of Proverbs in the Old Testament of the Bible contains a statement that is part of nearly every creed and faith: "Train a child in the way he should go, and when he is old, he will not turn from it." This verse places the highest priority on the need for parents to discipline their children so they will produce healthy, well-adjusted adults.

Remember, also, that children also learn by imitating. If you attend worship services, you will likely take your child for whatever age-appropriate activities are provided. If you are not a part of a church, how can you expect your child to be? Church sports leagues are particularly good for children who aren't skilled enough to play on school teams, and these leagues allow your child to experience success playing with those at their own level. In addition your son will learn social and team building skills. The coaches of these teams are also those who can serve as strong positive male role models.

All of the boys who go to church or take part in church activities are not perfect, but the chance of their being better students and better citizens is far more likely if they are a part of organized church activities. Most churches also have drama, music, activity clubs, and other activities that provide outlets for your son's interests.

The Book of Proverbs also includes "Discipline your son while there is hope," another statement that speaks to disciplining a child before he develops habits that will be hard for him to break. The sole purpose of discipline is to teach. If you discipline now, enforcing discipline as he grows older will not be as challenging. The longer children live without consistent and dedicated discipline the more unmanageable they usually become. What is *dedicated* discipline? The answer is *consistent* discipline as you raise your son. You will instill respect by raising him in an atmosphere of positive morality and values which foster positive behavior. Dedicated discipline gives him the boundaries he wants and needs.

Respect

The first element of dedicated discipline is teaching respect for you as his mother. This can begin as young as age 2. If your 2-year-old challenges you when you correct or instruct him, and he doesn't want to cooperate (typical of this age), you should be ready with the consequences that let him know that you are the parent, the adult, and the authority. At this point in his life, responding to his "Why?" with "Because I'm your mother, and I said so" makes perfectly good sense, and you must assert yourself as being the one who has the last word. You must win this battle of wills as early as possible.

Instilling *respect* should be the primary focus of your parenting, and discipline should be secondary. Demanding respect from your son when he is young will give him the framework during his pivotal, developmental years that guides the way he will treat authorities such as teachers, police officers, and other adults as he reaches adolescence and eventually adulthood.

If you wait to begin to demand respect until your son absolutely defies you, you will have a job on your hands if he is a 12-year old, for example. The older he becomes, the more difficult it will be to control him if he does not have the ability to discipline himself. If he develops into an adolescent and has defied you for 13 years, he will naturally continue to; however, his behavior can become much more serious when he is a bigger and stronger adolescent who is naturally seeking his identity and striving for his independence. The task of disciplining him in adolescence is very challenging. It can be done, but you will have to work very hard at being consistent with consequences and work towards being predictable to reduce his poor behaviors.

Consequences

You may be asking yourself how you can establish respect when your son has become so stubborn and defiant. Most people long for the perfect, peaceful, loving household with an established order of authority, but it takes work, and only consistent discipline will even begin to lead to this. Consequences are important in parenting because it teaches that for every action there is a response or reaction. For example if you treat your son with love, your son will most likely return it.

Sometimes mothers believe that consequences are too difficult to enforce, or their son may be going through a brief, turbulent stage which he will eventually outgrow. Others may even worry that their son will dislike them if they enforce discipline. This is not only completely false thinking, it will undoubtedly hurt him in the long run.

Let's take a closer look at why your son may misbehave. It may be to get attention, to get revenge, or because he needs a sense of control. The reasons for your son's misbehaviors may be caused by frustration, sickness, anger, disappointment, hunger, or fatigue, and he misbehaves as a reaction. Understanding the feelings or needs behind his behaviors will give you clues about how to handle them when they occur.

Parents usually present two kinds of consequences: *logical* and *natural.* Natural consequences are those things that happen naturally that help all of us learn how the world works—cause and effect. When your son was a toddler, you probably told him not to touch the stove. Being curious, he disobeyed and quickly discovered that the pretty flames hurt. Or maybe you told your son to wear his jacket when he went outside to play in the snow. He didn't wear the jacket, and in a few days, he told you he was feeling sick. That would have been a good time to explain to him that you were trying to protect him because becoming wet and cold can increase the likelihood of him being susceptible to illness. You can remind him of this the next time you tell him to wear his jacket when it is cold outside.

Logical consequences differ from *natural* consequences because logical consequences are determined by the one making the rules. If your son failed every subject, the logical consequence might be to remove a privilege he enjoys such as playing video games until you saw clear evidence of improved grades. Another example of a logical consequence with an older boy would be if he got a speeding ticket and had to appear in court. The court might impose a fine or loss of driving privileges for a specified time, so what might you do? Require him to pay the courts costs or more of the automobile insurance premium. A teenager who cannot drive is usually miserable and will certainly be eager to regain his driving privileges as soon as he possibly can.

Rules and the consequences of breaking them

Changing your son's behaviors require observing what he enjoys, planning what action to take, following through with action, and revising the plan as needed. Establishing consequences for unacceptable behavior tells him you care about him, particularly if you take time to explain the way you want him to live.

You must always make clear what the consequences are for not doing as you say he should do. If you tell him he must finish his dinner before he has dessert, stick to that. *Of course* it is easier to let him have the ice cream rather than put up with a loud, angry reaction, but don't change your mind. He had the **choice** of finishing his dinner, and he made the **choice** not to. He chose his own consequences.

You are the parent. Some parents are tangled in role reversals, with the child calling the shots and the parent giving in. Some mothers are frightened of disciplining an older son because they fear what he might do to her physically or to the house or another sibling in the household. A boy may try to take control because he believes his physical presence of greater size and strength will intimidate his mother.

If you fear what a young male might do, and you feel incapable of controlling him, call the police. *Caution*: **Do not ever threaten to do this unless** the behavior is indeed serious. If your son carries through with the action of physical violence, you MUST call the police because **you said you would.** If he does what you forbid and harms someone in the household, and you back down on the threat, he has control from then on. You will not be able to manage his behavior alone, and an outside authority or mental health professionals will have to be called in.

It depends on his age

Another rule to remember about consequences

is that they should be age appropriate. You should not discipline a 6-year-old as you would an adolescent for obvious reasons. Younger children need more direction because they have had far less experience reasoning through things, are still learning basic rules, and are naturally curious. Taking away the privileges of a 6-year-old for a week because he did not pick up his toys is unreasonable. A few hours of staying in while his friends play outside should suffice to make the point with a young child. You can, however, remove certain privileges for a week from your adolescent son if he breaks curfew after you told him what would happen if he came home late again.

Sometimes your son may misbehave because he is testing his limits. Children watch their mothers to see what their reaction might be after they have forbidden them to do something. It's the kind of thing that happens all the time in those old family movies and television shows: A boy is told not to touch the cookie jar because dinner is nearly ready. When his mother turns her back or is occupied by a phone call or someone at the door, he begins to move toward that cookie jar again. It is typical childish behavior, and few children will not try it.

The first time he does it or tries to do it, you should scold him and remind him that cookies are for dessert and that if he eats them, he will not be hungry for dinner, which is the food he needs. If he looks like he might try going for the cookie jar before dinner again, tell him what the consequences will be if you learn he has succeeded. Don't say, *"If you **try** that again"* because he may very well ***try it** and not be **caught**!* Remember, though, that it is normal for any child to try to get what he wants. What is important is that you do what you say you will do if he is caught with his "hand in the cookie jar" again!

You should always follow through with the consequences you set. I once observed a woman in a store scolding her 4-year-old son because he was carrying on loudly about wanting a piece of candy. She told him she would take him outside and punish him if he continued that behavior. He continued, and she begged and pleaded and even tried to reason him into stopping his screaming. Unfortunately, she did not take him outside or punish him in any other way that I could see, and eventually she gave in to his wishes. Her talk was all empty threats.

What would be more confusing to a child who gets his candy than to be later punished for his misbehavior in the store? He misbehaved and got his way. There is nothing reasonable a parent can do to punish him long after that the fact, but she can vow that she will not give in to him again, and she can tell him that not only will he not get what he is screaming for, he will be given consequences for his behavior.

Empty threats will certainly make your son believe that you are not to be taken seriously and that he can get away with whatever he wants to do. When you are consistent with your discipline, you become predictable, and your son will learn to trust you, learn to follow rules, and understand a lifelong lesson that he may not like the consequences if he breaks rules. What are effective ways to prevent rule breaking? Read on.

Principles of Dedicated Discipline
Rules
One of the first steps toward dedicated discipline is to establish rules in your household. They help to keep the family's environment consistent

and stable because everyone will know what is expected of him. Rules help to prevent chaos.

Making rules should be done as a family if at all possible. This means that everyone in the household should take part in setting rules that—of course—must be within reason.

Here are some examples of rules for all children.

1. No running in the house.
2. Follow the established curfew for school nights and holiday or weekend nights.
3. Do your share of household chores.
4. Complete homework before television or video games or talking to friends on the telephone.
5. Share computer or telephone use.
6. Take turns with both responsibilities and privileges.

Many other rules might be applicable to your household, and it should be easy to compose a list that suits your situation. Although rules help to enable a child to become responsible, you are the final authority. Make sure your son understands the rules and that they are clear. Have him explain them to you so you know with certainty that he understands.

Repetition

It is important to repeat instructions, as children—just like adults--tend to have selective hearing when it suits them. There cannot be a rule for every possible thing he does, so think of ways to classify them. The examples below represent two extremes of misbehavior that should not be treated with the same degree of punishment:

Serious: Physical harm to others, lying, cheating, and stealing merit serious consequences appropriate to your son's age.

Minor: A low grade on a report card (one D, for example), not coming inside when told to the first or second time, or having to be reminded every night to brush his teeth are far less serious, and consequences should be relatively mild.

When discussing rules, tell him that different families have different rules to follow. Your son will naturally compare himself with his friends and other families. Nearly all parents who have ever established a rule hear that they are not being fair because John does not have a curfew or Mike does not have to complete his homework before he goes outside.

The answers most adults remember their parents giving are, "This is our house, not John's, and we go by our own rules" or "You don't live in Mike's house." When negotiation in your household occurs and is not negotiable, you should probably say something similar. It has worked for centuries—even though children throughout the years have not been satisfied by it.

Remember that making a rule you really don't want to have to enforce could cause a great burden or inconvenience for you. If, for example, you punish your son by taking away driving privileges, you may have to take him to appointments or activities yourself. Don't establish a rule you don't want to have to enforce.

Praise him when he does what he is supposed to do—particularly when you don't have to ask him to do it (homework, dishes, taking out the trash, feeding the dog, or other things of that nature). If you want him to do what he is supposed to do, use praise to reinforce good behavior. It works far better than punishment does to prevent further negative behavior.

There are two final points about setting rules I would like you to remember:

1. Rules should change as your son develops throughout the years.

2. Establish rules only when you know you can and will enforce them.

Guidelines for effective discipline

Effective discipline should be guided by remembering that when you deal with your son, you should talk to him in a **friendly** (rather than impatient or angry) manner, that you should always be **fair** with him, and that you should be **firm** when you establish guidelines.

Friendly: Use a gentle rather than threatening manner when you discipline him. This does not mean you should smile when you punish him. It simply means that your facial expression and body language should not sound threatening. Let him know he will receive the consequences your family has established if he breaks the rules. It is important that he knows what he should do next time so he can avoid the punishment.

Fair: The punishment should fit the crime. Do not punish him for a month because he got a D on a spelling test. Your son needs to learn from his mistakes and not be treated like a prisoner. Appropriate consequences for a bad spelling test grade would be for you to require him to spell the words out loud to you once a day until he gets all of them correct. Removing privileges is effective when used consistently and the consequences have been established. Consistency equals predictability. If you are consistent, then your son will know the consequences for particular actions.

Firm: Don't give in to pleading. If he knows he will not be able to go to the mall with his friends if he doesn't take out the trash and cleans his room before 12p.m. and none of his chores are accomplished, then he does not go to the mall with his friends that day. You may have to put up with him sulking around the house while his friends are out, but next week the trash will probably be taken out regularly without a reminder. Sometimes a mother will have to endure something unpleasant for a while in order not to have to deal with a problem repeatedly.

Behavior Charts and Incentives

Behavior charts are visual aids that allow families to track their child's progress. You and your son can establish rewards for good behavior along with consequences for inappropriate behaviors.

I recommend behavior charts be used for a child as soon as he can read and be used through the elementary and middle school grades.

Older children tend to respond more favorably to incentives and contracts. A contract is simply a written document with your son that makes clear how he can earn something if he does certain things. Having the contract typed makes it look more official, but if it is handwritten, it must still be honored. You might even make multiple copies so you can put one on the refrigerator and so your son and you will each have a copy.

The following is an example of a contract. The important thing is that it establishes what behavior the boy has to achieve to get the reward he wants.

Behavior Contract

Starting date_____   Ending date_____
Month/Day/Year   Month/Date/Year

I, (_____son's name_____), pledge to earn no
grade lower than a B on my report card for the
third grading period. If I do, my mother will

_____

_____

_____

_____

(Suggested things might be *buy a video game for
me* **or** *let me go to the arcade once a week* **or** *spend
xxx hours a week at the skateboard park* **or** *have
friends over for a sleepover the following weekend.* The
important things are that **he chooses** whatever he
values most, within reason, and that you honor
that promise if he meets his obligations.)

_____

Mother's signature   Date

_____

Son's signature   Date

He can also help you to compose a behavior chart that gives him more responsibility for his actions and more motivation to participate in the program. It is important to keep rewards simple and to use them for one behavior at a time. Rewards can be as small as an ice cream cone or as large as a bicycle- - if both of you agree on them. Larger rewards should be reserved after appropriate behaviors are shown for a longer period of time. Here is an example of a behavioral chart you can use. Modify as needed for your home.

Son's name

	MON	TUES	WED	THURS	FRI	SAT	TOTALS
I followed directions.	AM PM	AM PM	AM PM	AM PM	AM PM	AM PM	
I cleaned my room.	AM PM	AM PM	AM PM	AM PM	AM PM	AM PM	
I did my homework.	AM PM	AM PM	AM PM	AM PM	AM PM	AM PM	
I was nice to my brother/ sister.	AM PM	AM PM	AM PM	AM PM	AM PM	AM PM	

28 out of 48 = earns the reward (Perfection is too much to ask for)

Incentive: I am earning a trip to an amusement park or some other reward.

Other positive reinforcers

Incentives or positive reinforcers can be specific activities, objects, or events which can be used to motivate a person for an action. Here are a few ideas of reinforcers to help you get started.

Food:

What does your son enjoy eating or drinking?

- Hamburgers, hot dogs, French fries, for example.

- Fruits, nuts, or cereal.

- Sweets or junk food: ice cream, cookies, or donuts.

What things does your son like to drink?

- Juices

- Soft drinks

- Milk

Praise: What kinds of praise and physical contact does your son like to receive from you or others?

- "Good boy."

- "I knew you could do it."

- "Great job."

- "Keep up the good work."

Physical contact

- Hugs

- Secret handshake

- High five

- Pat on the back

Activities: What activities does your son enjoy indoors?:

- Crafts

- Video games

- Having a friend over for the weekend

- Playing computer games

Outside:

- Fishing or hunting

- Activities that require money like going to a restaurant, amusement park, zoo, or a professional sports game.

- Activities that take time such as playing basketball or baseball, skateboarding,

Recreational reinforcers: What kinds of games or toys interest him?

- Toy cars

- Coloring books and crayons

- Video games

- DVDS and videos

- Stickers

If you look at these examples, you will be able to think of more activities that your son enjoys.

By using these reinforcers, you can help to significantly improve your son's behaviors by motivating him to reduce the negative, inappropriate behaviors you have discussed.

Timeouts

When people talk about a "timeout" as a consequence of certain behaviors, they are talking about removing a misbehaving child from an environment he was enjoying. In sports, timeouts are used to allow a team to confer with the coaches and with each other about the best strategy to use to win a game. When your son is in timeout, he is required to be still and quiet so that he can reestablish self-control. Likewise, you can use the time for yourself to cool down after having to deal with his behavior. Incidentally, timeouts work best for children aged 2-10. Adolescents are most effectively disciplined by depriving them of the company of their friends, removing privileges, and not giving them money.

The timeout does not begin until your child is absolutely quiet and free from distraction. He also needs to know how long the timeout will be. For children ages 6-8, you could watch the clock together, use a stopwatch, or count together to

60. If they are really young (2-5), you could use a kitchen timer or an hourglass, which can be purchased at a dollar store. Boys ages 9-10 can use their watches to know when their timeout ends.

Here is an example of how to manage an effective timeout. Donald, who is eight years old, is screaming and talking disrespectfully to his mother because she told him that he needed to finish his homework before he could watch cartoons.

"Donald, I told you to stop screaming," said his mother.

"I said no!" Donald screamed back at her.

"I will count to five, and after five if you haven't stopped screaming, you will sit at the kitchen table with me." She counted slowly "1-2-3-4-5." Donald continued to scream that he wanted to watch cartoons right then.

"All right, then, sit right down here."

"I will not! You can't tell me what to do!"

"If I count to five again, you will not only have to take a 10-minute timeout at the table, but you will go to bed 30 minutes early and cannot watch television tonight."

Why did she increase the consequences after he didn't obey her the first time? She did this because

Donald was testing her by becoming even more defiant, and the only way to convey the message of seriousness was to make the punishment more unpleasant. The mother in this illustration used her interventions effectively and was not manipulated by her son's behaviors. Notice, too, that she did not automatically add the additional consequences. She said, "**If** I count to five again."

Here are some important points to remember about timeouts.

1. They are effective when they are presented as a choice. Do so-and-so or don't do-so-and-so **or** you will get a timeout.

2. They are effective if you are persistent in removing privileges and adding consequences to stay in charge of the situation like the mother in the illustration did.

3. Follow up on the timeout by discussing with your son what he did that got him in the timeout in the first place and what he will do to make a better choice next time.

If your son sits quietly and has his feelings under control after the timeout, praise him or give him a hug for his good behavior. Mothers who say timeouts are ineffective, I believe, are simply giving up and relinquishing their parental authority to their sons.

Some mothers become frustrated by their son's manipulation and tell me that no form of discipline is effective. The simple reason this happens is that their sons have manipulated them. Children are highly adept at manipulation and have learned when they were quite young what they can do to get their way. Here are a few manipulative techniques I have seen children use with their mothers to get what they want and to distract their mothers from using consequences.

Guilt trips- "Mom, you treat me like a little kid! Ken doesn't have to this" or "You don't love me anymore" or "Everybody else is going. Why can't I?" In addition to the verbal manipulation, boys may also look sad and may even cry to get their mothers to give in to their demands.

Tantrums - These are when your son yells and screams in hopes you may become so frustrated or distracted you will eventually back off. It can also involve lying on the floor and kicking his feet on the floor or in the air as he yells.

Ignoring you - This is also called "selective hearing." Your son acts as if he did not hear you, hoping you will eventually forget what you were telling him to do.

Extreme defiance - Telling you he refuses to do something you asked and challenges you to make him do it. This is done to frighten you.

Whining - "Can't you do this for me? This is too *hard*." He says these things so you feel guilty, and instead of him doing what he is supposed to do, you give in and do it yourself.

Threatening - "I'm going to run away from home if you take my video games away!" "I hate you and everything about this house, so I might as well kill myself!"

Some boys tend to use threatening as a last resort when their mothers ignore the other manipulations. One technique that nearly always works is as follows: If your son says he is running away from home, tell him you will call the police as soon as he leaves the house to ensure he is safe and that you will send his picture to the local and community newspapers and post pictures of him in the neighborhood. You can also tell him you will offer a cash reward to be paid out of his own money if anyone reports his whereabouts. If he threatens to kill himself, you can say, "Experts say to take every threat of suicide seriously, so if I hear that again, I'll have to take you to a doctor for a mental health evaluation. He may decide that you will need to stay in a hospital until you are not suicidal anymore."

When your son makes threats, it is to force you to give in to his demands. If he threatens to run away or kill himself when you deny him something he wants to do, he is trying to manipulate you. If you give in, his threats are working because he gets what he wants, and you can be sure he will try them again. There is a danger that one day he will follow through on these threats, so it is critical that you stop this behavior early.

Remember that firmness, consistency, and repetition are all necessary if you are to implement dedicated discipline. Almost all children can be challenging and difficult to rear at every developmental stage, but the rewards are great when they do succeed because of your child rearing. You know the joy you feel when your son has accomplished something that is commendable.

Here are some key points to remember about consequences:

1. Be open and willing to try new things.

2. Listen and observe before taking action.

3. Choose consequences that are appropriate and fit the action.

4. Be consistent and follow through.

All parents make mistakes, and so will you. You can only try to be consistent, loving, and willing to learn, as parenting is a continual learning process. A single mother has an even more daunting task of parenting because she is in it by herself and often has to rely on her own resources because she lacks a partner in the process. Remember that discipline is a form of teaching to help your son develop into a responsible and productive man. Do not expect to be a perfect mother, but strive to be the best you can because what you are doing is the most important job there is.

7

MODELING, MENTORING, AND MALE ROLE MODELS

Single mothers are often frustrated by the ways their sons handle their feelings. One reported that her adolescent boy destroyed things in his bedroom and even damaged the furniture when he was frustrated with her. Ironically, however, she told me that she had damaged the television set beyond use in the past because she was frustrated with her son, whom she said showed disrespect and "provoked" her.

Modeling Behavior

It should come as no surprise to anyone that whatever a parent does, the child is likely to imitate. Some adults drink and smoke, and these practices are touted by the alcohol and tobacco in-

dustries as "adult" choices. And what entices an underage adolescent more than wanting to look like
an adult? A child is told not to curse, but adults do,
so children equate that with "adult" behavior. And
what child or adolescent doesn't want to be *grown*
as soon as possible?

The apple doesn't fall far from the tree, and if
children handle problems the way their parents
do, what behavior could be more natural? Why
wouldn't a parent expect the child to act as the
adults in his home act? So much has been said
of positive "role models" in our culture—people
who "model" the kind of behavior young people
should aspire to emulate. Yet many parents say
"*Do as I **say**, not as I **do**,*" but it is not realistic to
expect a boy to be *more* mature, *more* rational,
more in control of his emotions than his mother
is. It is terribly unfair to a child to expect him to
be an adult when there is no one for him to turn
to or if his mother does not give him positive and
consistent guidance. Have you ever considered
that giving an out-of-control boy a hug might
vaporize his anger in an instant and that it might
be the warm, human contact *you* also need.

It is important for you to show your son how to

handle difficult situations. If you are frustrated or angry, don't let your son see your temper get out of control. Learn to handle your own frustrations by finding ways to deal with it in healthy ways: leave the house and take a walk, exercise, call a friend to discuss the problem or any other healthy way to redirect your frustration. By acting in these constructive ways, your son will learn that under stress and pressure you can manage your feelings. This is what is known as "modeling" appropriate behavior.

A son learns from observing your actions and modeling or imitating them. This, unfortunately, includes your *bad* as well as your *good* habits. If you smoke cigarettes or curse, your son is far more likely to smoke cigarettes or use profane language because his mother does. Mothers who seek professional help to get their sons to stop smoking or cursing, but who smoke at home or curse while they are in my office, are being self-defeating. If you want your child to exhibit positive behavior, you must do the same. He will imitate both your good *and* bad qualities as he struggles to define himself as the kind of person he thinks he wants to become. I would like to devote the rest of this chapter to the importance of male mentorship.

The importance of male mentors in your son's life cannot be underestimated. Children who have mentors are almost half as likely to use illegal drugs, almost a third less likely to use alcohol, and only half as likely to skip school than kids who don't have mentors. Kids with mentors also report that they are more confident of their school performance, more likely to get along with others, and less likely to hit someone.[10]

No matter how much you want to see things from your son's viewpoint, a woman cannot fully understand how it is to be a boy or man. She has never had any experiences as a male, and the pressures and hormones and cultural expectations of the genders are quite different. Whether this situation is right or wrong or fair is beside the point. The differences in the cultural expectations of boys and girls in our world are simply facts. Those differences are the most important reasons a male mentor is vitally important for your son. He needs someone he can relate to and identify with and talk to about things that are outside the realm of a woman's experience.

Just the fact of being older and a male does *not*

necessarily make a man the mentor you want for your son. A good male mentor must be someone you know and trust fully who will be a model for his development as a man. A relative such as a grandfather or male cousin or uncle should probably be considered first because you already have a good sense of who they are and what they are about. You can also consider a male friend or neighbor who also shares your values.

But what if there are no males in your family or other acquaintances you believe would be the right person for your son? You may find male mentors through a church, school, recreational league, Boy Scouts, or Big Brothers. Local houses of worship have pastors or youth leaders or other reputable men you can trust your son with. They could also have connections with upstanding members of the community who would be willing to give your son their friendship or guidance. The influences of a young man's association with a church can also have the potential to create relationships and spiritual experiences which can impact his world for a lifetime.

If you find a good male mentor, you need to have some assurance that he will give your son regular time the boy can count on. If you cannot get a firm commitment from a mentor for a few days or a few times a month, your son may be in the same position he was when he lost his father—not having a man to count on to be there when he needs a man's advice.

Your son's school is also a resource for male mentorship. Male teachers often work as club advisors or sponsor groups of boys in various after-school programs. A school principal should be able to offer suggestions about the kinds of activities that are available and whether there are any males connected to the school who might want to mentor a boy.

Boy Scouts, although it may not be considered as cool as hanging out at the video arcade, is a good place for a boy to make friends and be led by men who can mentor him. If he joins Cub Scouts as early as first grade, he will have wholesome activities to participate in all through elementary school. Boy Scouts begins at age 11 or in grade 6, and some men remain in scouting in some way or another all of their lives. Scouting provides leaders who are interested in boys' well-being who will give them opportunities to learn leadership and survival skills.

Another source of male leaders is Big Brothers. Its purpose is to match boys who need a relationship with an older male who wants to help a boy. A single mother I counseled was having tremendous problems raising her son because he missed his father so much. His emotional problems were causing significant difficulty in the classroom as well as at home. A call to Big Brothers led to finding a match with a big brother. His mother reported a change in his mood and behavior after just a few weeks, which astonished her.

Such a swift and dramatic turnaround in his behavior showed how vital it was for her son to have male mentorship, even though I am convinced that his mother was a good parent who was trying her best to raise him alone. Big Brothers has an excellent record of helping boys: Little Brothers are half as likely to skip school, nearly half as likely to begin using illegal drugs, and usually get along with their families and peers better than those who don't have a Big Brother.[11] That track record should be encouragement for you to seek the help of this organization.

A Few Cautions

You should get to know any potential mentor you select for your son. You need to know what his beliefs and values are, as your son will be influenced by his beliefs and values. Although it is unpleasant to mention here, there are men, even ministers, teachers, coaches, and scout leaders who molest boys. If your son seems depressed or anxious after being with his mentor, ask him what is wrong. If he doesn't want to talk about it, **assure him you will believe what he tells you**. If he says he is being touched inappropriately, or if you smell liquor on his breath, or if his behavior is erratic, contact the social service agency.

Although there are certainly sick people out there who prey on children, don't let what you read or see on television prevent you from trying to find a male mentor who can be a positive guide and companion for your son. What you must do to assure yourself that he will not harm your boy is to get to know him first or talk with people you trust who know him.

The purpose of social service agencies is to help people like you and your son. If you need their help, they should be eager to give it. Don't give up until your son has a male he can trust who will give him time.

8
LOOKING AHEAD

I have stated throughout the book that single parenthood will multiply the degree of stress in a family. Because you have the full-time job of raising a son, in addition to all of your other tasks, you probably do not have the time for yourself that every individual needs. No mother wants to shortchange her child with too little attention, but if she neglects her own needs, her mental and physical health can suffer. As a result, she will be less able to do an effective job of parenting, so her efforts will be minimized.

Some mothers feel they have to spend all of their energy solely on child rearing. This can increase their problems, including resenting the child who takes so much time. They can also ignore things that are really essential to their personal needs. The truth is that if you don't take good care of yourself, you will not be able to take the best care of a child.

This book has been aimed at helping you to raise a successful son alone. You, however, are the most vital person in this task. What could be more fitting than to end this book with things you can do to take care of yourself. Because raising children demands a lot of physical and emotional energy, taking care of yourself is essential. You are not only raising your son by yourself, you may have other children, in addition to job and financial pressures. All of these add to the demands of single parenting.

It may be difficult and challenging for you to take care of yourself because your mothering instinct may cause you to neglect your own needs. When you neglect yourself and put yourself last, your behavior suggests that a person is important only when he or she is providing service to others. It is important to give to others, but if you also take care of yourself, your son will see that both of you are important and have important needs. Still, no one has more than 24 hours in a day, so what can you do to change? How can you have time for yourself that will allow you to develop a positive lifestyle every day?

There are many ways you can help yourself, but here are *five practical* suggestions you can do for yourself to take care of yourself. Nearly every woman, regardless of her circumstances or lifestyle or age, can follow them.

Sleep

Many individuals have trouble sleeping at night because they are under great stress or worry excessively. However, good quality sleep is necessary for our minds and bodies to function normally. Sleepiness during the day from not getting enough sleep at night is an emerging problem in the United States and affects a number of adults.

I am sure you have seen the number of television commercials and media advertisements about the use of sleeping medications to obtain better sleep. You may wisely require your son to go to bed so that he can get enough sleep, but are you following that routine yourself? Stress is usually a contributing factor when adults are sleep deprived, but if adequate sleep is obtained, stress is reduced.

It is recommended that adults sleep 7-8 hours each night, but how can you get this amount of sleep if stress is keeping you awake? It sounds like a problem without a solution. There are, however, a number of ways to improve the quality of your sleep if you cannot get the hours you need.

First, you will need to establish a regular sleep schedule. One way to achieve this is to avoid taking naps during the day. Even though you may be tired, it is best you go to bed earlier rather than take a nap because a nap will postpone the time you are sleepy enough to go to bed. Secondly, avoid caffeine and alcohol for at least 4 hours before bedtime. Coffee, teas and sodas contain caffeine which may keep you awake. Likewise, do not drink alcohol to help you sleep.

We all know about the effects of alcohol psychologically, physically, and physiologically on an individual. However, some individuals claim that alcohol can help to reduce insomnia. Alcohol may help you fall asleep initially; however, as your body clears it from your system, alcohol can cause sweating, headaches, and nightmares that will cause sleep disturbances. Thus, it is not a good idea to use alcohol as a sleep aid or for a coping intervention.

It is also not a good idea to use television to help you fall asleep. Some people use television as a sleeping aid, but watching television tends to keep your attention on the program and delays the time you fall asleep. If you insist that you need to listen to something to help you fall asleep, use a radio and listen to soothing music that relaxes you. There are also many compact disks containing various sounds specifically designed to relax you and help you sleep better. You may want to check your local store to browse them. When people get less sleep, even one hour less than they need each night, they can develop many problems. Being sleep deprived can lead to poor performance and concentration, memory lapses, accidents and injuries, irrational thinking, and mood problems. It can even cause you to fall asleep at inappropriate (in meetings or on the job) or even dangerous (operating machinery or automobiles) times. Remember that sleep is necessary for optimal mental, emotional, and physical functioning!

Eating a healthy diet

One of the most disturbing—and avoidable--public health problems in the 21st century is obesity. Not only are the numbers increasing, but overweight people are becoming even heavier. This condition usually begins in childhood. It is rarely from a glandular problem or "big bones," but instead is from poor nutrition choices.

If a child is given food that contains what are called "empty calories" like salty, greasy snacks or sweets, those will become the choices the child makes as he becomes older. So you have to model appropriate eating habits for your child. "Fast food" meals also contribute to weight gain. The typical taco or burger is loaded with fat and refined white flour. To make it tastier, the restaurant also adds a lot of salt. These ingredients, in excess, add pounds and also contribute to many diseases such as hypertension and high cholesterol that could probably be avoided if a person ate healthy foods.

Single mothers who are employed outside the home often tell me they don't have enough time to prepare meals and do all of the other tasks they have to do to manage their household. They pick up take-out because it's easy, and their children will eat it. This is understandable, but eating habits can last a lifetime, and it is important to try to make time for planning healthy meals while children are young. Children who are fed healthy food at an early age will choose healthy food as adults.

Some mothers cope with stress by eating, and their weight increase will often contribute to more stress and can lead to disease. They may worry about the weight or have increased blood pressure or develop heart conditions. Diabetes is also associated with unhealthy eating habits. Single mothers tend to have greater stress than those in two-parent households, and sometimes will say such statements like "Eating is the only thing I enjoy," so they indulge themselves in eating too much.

The healthiest way to be slim is not to let yourself gain the extra weight in the first place—but that is not useful advice after the weight is already there. Drinking a lot of water--six to eight glasses a day is recommended--and eating small portions helps. Eating fruits and vegetables instead of sugary snacks will also help you stay on track with your weight. Reducing your intake of fried food (french fries, chicken, onion rings) and limiting meals at fast food restaurants will both lower your caloric intake and enhance your bank account. It costs more to eat out than it does to make meals from raw ingredients.

Unfortunately, there is no easy fix for losing a lot of weight gained over a long period. Fad diets may seem to work at first, but health risks are associated with many of them. Some require you to do without some kinds of foods, but your body needs a broad spectrum of vitamins, minerals, and other elements to work efficiently. If you are tired, not only do you lack energy, but your body will crave quick-energy food like sugar. This leads to the next important recommendation.

Getting regular exercise

Not too many people like to exercise, but it is one of the most important things you can do for overall physical and mental health. The benefits of exercise are numerous. It increases your metabolism so that you burn more calories, helps you to sleep better, gives you more energy, increases the strength of your bones, and lowers your blood pressure. It also increases circulation so that more blood flows to your skin. That will make you look and feel healthier. In fact, you will **be** healthier.

Gym membership can be expensive, but you don't need a gym to exercise. Walking in the neighborhood, at a public track or at a school, at a mall, or using a workout video (available at public libraries) to exercise are also ways to make exercise convenient and practical. There are even television programs that lead a viewer through routines designed to increase fitness.

The benefits of exercise are so many that you should try to find a way to incorporate it into your daily routine or at least a few times a week. Recent studies at Duke University found that exercising one hour, three times a week, can be as effective for improving emotional health as taking an antidepressant. It is also free and better for you!

Forming and keeping friendships

Everyone should develop and maintain a social network of friends for outings and to talk with. This social network enables you to spend time with people your own age and talk about "adult" issues instead of being with children most of the time. Single parenting can be very lonely, so try to cultivate strong friendships with those you know you can trust to watch your son so you can take a break and enjoy adult company. Be willing to take turns with these responsibilities so your friends have you to count on as well. Having friends to spend time with also alleviates the stress of loneliness.

If you can spend a little time to become involved in community or church activities or service organizations, you will be in an environment where you meet other adults. Your participation and involvement also show your son that community activities are important. Remember, too, that when you have a network of adult friends, you increase the chances of meeting a male who might be a mentor to your son or a companion to you.

Paying attention to your mental health

Seeing a mental health therapist such as a counselor or psychologist for additional support is often valuable. People used to think and some still do believe that if you go to a therapist, you must have serious mental problems. Many people wouldn't seek the help they needed because of that attitude and stigma. That false notion has driven away many who need therapy from getting help to overcome whatever difficulty they were experiencing.

A mental health professional not only listens, but can suggest many ways for you to deal with your problems and overcome them. This person can serve as a support to you as you raise your son and will teach and encourage you to use self-talk when you are feeling frustrated.

Some examples of self-talk for a parent are

"I know my son is trying to gain control over my emotions, so I will stay calm."

"I can raise him without a man to help me."

"I don't like this situation, but I can handle it."

"I will not raise my voice or strike him even if he makes me angry." These are only a few examples of self-talk that can help you in times of stress when parenting.

Developing a spiritual life

I need to mention the power of prayer to help you in your parenting. Prayer gives many people the strength they need to meet the challenges of life. Here is an example of a short prayer you can say to rededicate yourself to becoming a better parent. Say it to yourself any time you need to—no matter where you are or when you think of it:

Thank you, God, for my son. Help me to love him unconditionally. Give me the wisdom and patience to parent him well, and help him to develop into a mature, responsible man.

This prayer and the statements above will help to give you the confidence to do what you need to do to stay in control of the situation, your emotions, and your actions. A mental health professional may also help you with expressing your feelings through journaling and writing. These interventions are therapeutic and can help you see in writing your past struggles and how you have been improving. These writings could be shared with your therapist or kept private.

Creating a Parenting Plan

Parents almost always know the things they do in anger or spontaneously when they discipline their children. Some hit, some yell, some send the child from the room without any discussion. Most parents recognize it when they have made bad choices and regret their actions. As you review in your mind the most recent ways you have dealt with your child's misbehavior, make a list of your responses. This will help you to see patterns and to recognize the effects of your methods.

This list leads to my last suggestion, something I call a *parenting plan*. After having read the advice in this book, you should be able to create a list of ways you want to change your own behavior in order to change your son's behavior. Create a list similar to the one that follows and carry it with you or keep it where you can read it as needed. Strive to keep the promises every day, and congratulate yourself if you can stick to your list. Some items may have to be altered, and you can always add more.

Parenting Plan

Today I will try to do the following things if my son misbehaves:

1. Give him timeouts.

2. Take away electronic toys or games.

3. Restrict his telephone use.

4. Limit computer use to schoolwork.

5. Not let him play with friends after school.

6. Restrict his television viewing time.

In the past, I have reacted to problems by

1. Screaming or nagging.

2. Spanking or slapping him in anger.

3. Threatening to do things I did not follow through with.

Here is what I plan to do differently:

1. Be consistent and firm with punishment.

2. Not let him talk me into giving in.

3. Keep control of my emotions and stay calm.

4. Not touch him when I am angry.

A list such as this, tailored to your personal situation, can keep you focused on improving your parenting.

We know that boys benefit from a father's guidance, but I have illustrated throughout the book that you can be mother and father if you must be. If you follow my suggestions and are not afraid to ask for help if you need it, you can raise a son who is confident, happy, and successful.

Try to devote as much time and energy as you can to giving your son the richest and most satisfying childhood possible. He will grow into manhood before you know it, and you will not be able to recapture those younger years and do things over again. I hope this book has convinced you that you can be a single parent and raise a son successfully. I know you can.

SOURCES OF HELP AND INFORMATION

Single Parenting

Single Parent Resource Center

Suite 200

31 E. 28th Street

New York, NY 10016-9998

(212) 951-7030

http://singleparentusa.com

Single Parent USA has information on single parent organizations in the United States and around the world. Its goal is to enable single parent groups and organizations to share information on program development, provide service models and techniques, and facilitate referral of single parents to groups or support programs in their local communities.

National Organization of Single Mothers, Inc.

P. O. Box 68

Midland, NC 28107

(704) 888-5437

http://www.singlemothers.org

This is the official site of the National Organization of Single Mothers, Inc., dedicated to helping single mothers encounter the daily challenges of life with invaluable information and various resources.

Parents Without Partners (PWP International Headquarters)

Suite 510

1650 S. Dixie Highway

Boca Raton, FL 33432

(561) 391-8833

http://parentswithoutpartners.org

Parents Without Partners provides single parents and their children with an opportunity for enhancing personal growth, self-confidence by offering an environment for support, friendship and the exchange of parenting techniques.

M.O.M.S., the international non-profit organization for all single parents, is dedicated to providing assistance to the single parent family: single mothers, single fathers, widows, widowers, and grandparents.

> M.O.M.S.
>
> Suite 6-176
>
> 475 College Blvd.
>
> Oceanside, CA 92057-5512
>
> phone: (760) 726-7978
>
> fax: (760) 726-7712
>
> http://www.singlemoms.org/

SingleRose.com is a site designed for divorced, widowed, and never-married women raising children alone. There are articles on various of topics of interest to single mothers.

> SingleRose.com
>
> P.O. Box 487
>
> Kennedale, TX 76060
>
> http://www.singlerose.com/

The Single Parent Network

> http://www.makinglemonade.com

Offers a wealth of information for the single mother.

Child Rearing

> http://www.todaysparent.com provides a number of resources on child rearing.
>
> Focus on the Family
>
> http://www.family.org is the focus on the family

website. This site provides a number of resources on child discipline and single parenting.

Mental Health

Focus Adolescent Resources helps one to find resources on adolescent and family issues http://www.focusas.com/Resources.html

American Academy of Child and Adolescent Psychiatry

Information to aid in the understanding and treatment of the developmental, behavioral, and mental disorders that affect children and adolescents http://www.aacap.org

Mentoring

Big Brothers/Big Sisters matches those who volunteer to mentor young people with those who need a mentor.

www.bigbrothersbigsisters.org

The Boy Scouts of America can provide information about local Boy Scouts organizations in your area.

http://www.scouting.org

REFERENCES

1. S. Ventura and C. Bachrach, *Non-marital Child-bearing in the United States*, 1940-1999. National Center for Health Statistics. (National Vital Statistics Reports: Hyattsville, MD, 2000): 48.

2. National Center for Fathering, Fathering in America Poll, January 1999.

3. J. Wallerstein, J. M. Lewis, and S. Blakeslee. *The Unexpected Legacy of Divorce: A Twenty-Five Year Landmark Study.* (New York: Hyperion, 2000).

4. National Fatherhood Initiative. Retrieved July 23, 2006, from http//www.fatherhood.org/fatherfacts

5. E. Hetherington. "Divorce and the Adjustment of Children." *Pediatrics in Review* 26 (2005):163-169.

6. D. Newton. *Teen Violence out of Control.* (Springfield, NJ: Enslow, 1995).

7. D. Baumrind, "Current Patterns of Parental Authority." *Developmental psychology monographs* (1971): 4.

-------------- "New Directions in Socialization Research." *Psychological Bulletin 1980*; 35: 639-652.

8. L. Johnston, J. Bachman, and P. O'Malley. *Monitoring the Future Study.* (Lansing, MI: University of Michigan, 2000).

9. Kaiser Family Foundation. Retrieved May 15, 2006, from www.kff.org

10. J. P. Tierney, J. B. Grossman, and N. L. Resch. *Making a Difference: An Impact Study of Big Brothers Big Sisters.* (Philadelphia: Public/Private Ventures, 1995).

11. http://www.bbbs.org/site/c.diJKKYPLJvH/b.1539751/k.BDB6/Home.htm

16720043R00083

Made in the USA
Lexington, KY
07 August 2012